SEX·TIPS

❖FROM❖

1894

SEX TIPS FROM 1894

First published in 2008
This edition copyright © Summersdale Publishers Ltd, 2023

An Hachette UK Company
www.hachette.co.uk

Summersdale Publishers Ltd
Part of Octopus Publishing Group Limited
Carmelite House
50 Victoria Embankment
LONDON
EC4Y 0DZ
UK

www.summersdale.com

Printed and bound in Poland

ISBN: 978-1-83799-270-6

Substantial discounts on bulk quantities of Summersdale books are available to corporations, professional associations and other organizations. For details contact general enquiries: telephone: +44 (0) 1243 771107 or email: enquiries@summersdale.com.

✧ RUTH SMYTHERS ✧

SEX TIPS

CLIMAX
YLANG·YLANG
✧
DELICATE·LASTING

✧ FROM ✧

1894

THE SECRET TO A HAPPY MARRIAGE,
AS TOLD BY THE VICTORIANS

summersdale

INSTRUCTION
AND ADVICE
FOR THE YOUNG BRIDE

on the Conduct and
Procedure of the Intimate
and Personal Relationships
of the Marriage State
for the Greater Spiritual
Sanctity of this
Blessed Sacrament
and the Glory of God

By
Ruth Smythers
beloved wife of
The Reverend L. D. Smythers
Pastor of the Arcadian
Methodist Church of the
Eastern Regional Conference
Published in the year
of our Lord 1894
Spiritual Guidance Press
New York City

To the sensitive young woman who has had the benefits of proper upbringing, the wedding day is, ironically, both the happiest and most terrifying day of her life.

On the positive side, there
is the wedding itself, in
which the bride is the central
attraction in a beautiful and
inspiring ceremony...

... symbolizing her triumph
in securing a male to
provide for all her needs
for the rest of her life.

On the negative side, there is the wedding night, during which the bride must pay the piper, so to speak, by facing for the first time the terrible experience of sex.

At this point, dear reader,
let me concede one
shocking truth:

Some young women
actually anticipate the
wedding night ordeal with
curiosity and pleasure!
Beware such an attitude!

A selfish and sensual husband
can easily take advantage of
such a bride. One cardinal
rule of marriage should
never be forgotten:

GIVE LITTLE,
GIVE SELDOM,
AND ABOVE ALL,
GIVE GRUDGINGLY.

Otherwise what could have
been a proper marriage could
become an orgy of sexual lust.

On the other hand, the bride's
terror need not be extreme.
While sex is at best revolting
and at worst rather painful...

... it has to be endured, and
has been by women since
the beginning of time, and
is compensated for by the
monogamous home and by the
children produced through it.

It is useless, in most cases,
for the bride to prevail
upon the groom to forego
the sexual initiation.

While the ideal husband would
be one who would approach
his bride only at her request
and only for the purpose of
begetting offspring, such
nobility and unselfishness
cannot be expected from
the average man.

Most men, if not denied,
would demand sex
almost every day.

The wise bride will permit a
maximum of two brief sexual
experiences weekly during
the first months of marriage.

As time goes by she should make every effort to reduce this frequency.

Feigned illness, sleepiness, and headaches are among the wife's best friends in this matter.

Arguments, nagging, scolding, and bickering also prove very effective, if used in the late evening about an hour before the husband would normally commence his seduction.

Clever wives are ever on
the alert for new and better
methods of denying and
discouraging the amorous
overtures of the husband.

A good wife should expect to
have reduced sexual contacts
to once a week by the end of
the first year of marriage and
to once a month by the end
of the fifth year of marriage.

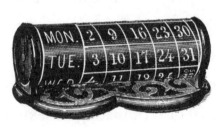

By their tenth anniversary many wives have managed to complete their child bearing and have achieved the ultimate goal of terminating all sexual contacts with the husband.

By this time she can depend upon his love for the children and social pressures to hold the husband in the home.

Just as she should be ever alert
to keep the quantity of sex
as low as possible, the wise
bride will pay equal attention
to limiting the kind and
degree of sexual contacts.

Most men are by nature
rather perverted, and if given
half a chance, would engage
in quite a variety of the
most revolting practices.

These practices include, among others: performing the normal act in abnormal positions; mouthing the female body; and offering their own vile bodies to be mouthed in turn.

Nudity, talking about
sex, reading stories about
sex, viewing photographs
and drawings depicting
or suggesting sex are the
obnoxious habits the male is
likely to acquire if permitted.

A wise bride will make it the
goal never to allow her husband
to see her unclothed body,
and never allow him to display
his unclothed body to her.

Sex, when it cannot be
prevented, should be practised
only in total darkness.

Many women have found it
useful to have thick cotton
nightgowns for themselves and
pyjamas for their husbands.
These should be donned in
separate rooms. They need
not be removed during the
sex act. Thus, a minimum
of flesh is exposed.

Once the bride has donned
her gown and turned off
all the lights, she should lie
quietly upon the bed and
await her groom. When
he comes groping into the
room she should make no
sound to guide him in her
direction, lest he take this as
a sign of encouragement.

She should let him grope in the dark. There is always the hope that he will stumble and incur some slight injury which she can use as an excuse to deny him sexual access.

When he finds her, the
wife should lie as still as
possible. Bodily motion on
her part could be interpreted
as sexual excitement by
the optimistic husband.

If he attempts to kiss her
on the lips she should turn
her head slightly so that
the kiss falls harmlessly
on her cheek instead.

If he attempts to kiss her
hand, she should make a fist.

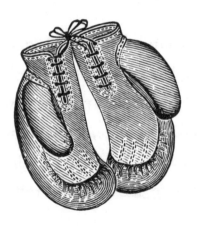

If he lifts her gown and attempts
to kiss her any place else she
should quickly pull the gown
back in place, spring from
the bed, and announce that
nature calls her to the toilet.

This will generally dampen
his desire to kiss in the
forbidden territory.

If the husband attempts to
seduce her with lascivious talk,
the wise wife will suddenly
remember some trivial
non-sexual question
to ask him.

MENU

Once he answers she should
keep the conversation going,
no matter how frivolous it
may seem at the time.

Eventually, the husband will learn that if he insists on having sexual contact, he must get on with it without amorous embellishment.

The wise wife will allow
him to pull the gown up no
farther than the waist, and
only permit him to open
the front of his pyjamas to
thus make connection.

She will be absolutely
silent or babble about her
housework while he is huffing
and puffing away. Above
all, she will lie perfectly
still and never under any
circumstances grunt or groan
while the act is in progress.

As soon as the husband
has completed the act, the
wise wife will start nagging
him about various minor
tasks she wishes him to
perform on the morrow.

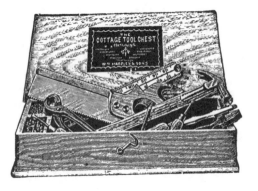

Many men obtain a major
portion of their sexual
satisfaction from the peaceful
exhaustion immediately
after the act is over.

Thus the wife must insure that
there is no peace in this period
for him to enjoy. Otherwise,
he might be encouraged
to soon try for more.

One heartening factor for which the wife can be grateful is the fact that the husband's home, school, church, and social environment have been working together all through his life to instil in him a deep sense of guilt in regards to his sexual feelings...

... so that he comes to the
marriage couch apologetically
and filled with shame, already
half cowed and subdued.

The wise wife seizes upon
this advantage and relentlessly
pursues her goal first to
limit, later to annihilate
completely her husband's
desire for sexual expression.

Have you enjoyed this book? If so, find us on
Facebook at **Summersdale Publishers**, on
Twitter at **@Summersdale** and on Instagram
and TikTok at **@summersdalebooks** and
get in touch. We'd love to hear from you!

www.summersdale.com

Image credits

Cover images: text © Mott Jordan/Shutterstock.com;
border © Extezy/Shutterstock.com; pp.1, 3 © Reinke Fox/
Shutterstock.com; pp.5, 9–10, 12, 14, 16, 18–20, 22, 24, 26,
28–30, 32, 34, 36, 38, 40, 42, 44, 46, 48, 50, 52, 54, 56,
58, 60, 62, 64, 66, 68, 70, 72, 74, 76, 78, 80–82, 84, 86,
88, 90, 92, 94, 96 © candycatdesigns/Shutterstock.com;
all the other images are public domain/out of copyright.